What Others Have Said About
GESTAPO CROWS: HOLOCAUST POEMS

Brodsky's poetic perspective on the Holocaust is at once unique, courageous and powerful. To capture all of this in verse is a remarkable achievement.
> — Harry James Cargas, author of *Reflections of a Post-Auschwitz Christian* and *A Christian Response to the Holocaust*

Gestapo Crows, like the painfully sharp metaphor of its title poem, builds upon Louis Daniel Brodsky's previous Holocaust collection, which he coauthored with William Heyen, *Falling from Heaven: Holocaust Poems of a Jew and a Gentile*. In *Gestapo Crows*, Brodsky continues his admirable struggle as a Jew and a highly gifted poet to fulfill what he calls his "second-generation 'survivor's' responsibility for dealing with the universal legacy of human cruelty and malevolence." This latest collection establishes Brodsky not only as a first-rate poet, but a poet who is struggling mightily to come to terms with his Jewishness through the powerful medium of his distinctive poetic voice.
> — Robert A. Cohn, Editor-in-Chief/Publisher, *St. Louis Jewish Light*

The disintegration of a contemporary American family. The suffering of the Jews in the death camps. How are these two events related? What do they have in common? And where is the suffering greater? I have never seen these startling questions posed in such a personal and convincing way. The poems in this book are shocking in their explicit detail. But more shocking — devastating really — is Brodsky's personal commandeering of historical events in order to illuminate and understand his own personal life. Doing that was a great risk and succeeding is Brodsky's great triumph.
> — Gregory Curtis, Editor of The 1991 National Magazine Award-winning *Texas Monthly*

I have received your book of Holocaust poems, and was very moved to read it. You are to be congratulated.
> — Martin Gilbert, author of *The Holocaust: A History of the Jews of Europe During the Second World War* and *Churchill: A Life*

Louis Daniel Brodsky has found a powerful subject — arguably *the* powerful twentieth century subject — or perhaps one should rightly say the subject has found him, clinging with its horrible relentlessness. To contend with it, Brodsky the poet has found power of his own, power that holds this subject in the tricky net of artistry and language. A disturbing, brave book.

> — Albert Goldbarth, author of ***Popular Culture, Arts & Sciences***, and the National Book Critics Circle Award-winning ***Heaven and Earth: A Cosmology***

I've read *Gestapo Crows* several times over, and it's dangerous stuff. You flay the sensibilities with a passion that is glaring, blindingly white in honesty; one that will not weaken with time. An emotional bloodbath. Searing. And paid for by you. That's plain. I tried all the critical approaches I know, and they didn't work. The absolute vulnerability conjoined to the repetitive power of your language is overwhelming. Your stuff is like patented moral medicine that must be taken in small doses. And now I'll tell you a secret that you cannot tell yourself, although the truth comes whispering to you in quiet moments: *You are an Old Testament prophet.* Period. Your stuff is too brutally honest to be fully appreciated in a situationally ethical time. Time is on your side. You've created a whole moral world that will slowly come into being.

> — Ted Hirschfield, author of ***Human Weather*** and ***German Requiem: Poems of the War and the Atonement of a Third Reich Child***

What Anselm Kiefer has done in his elaborate, haunting paintings recalling Nazi Germany, L.D. Brodsky has done in words no less elaborate and haunting. Perhaps the centerpiece of this collection of Holocaust memories is the poem called "Kafkaesque Vestiges, Germany, 1941," with its overriding image of Germany as the huge penal colony machine. Kafka hovers over the entire volume, and, like the novelist, the poet creeps into our individual histories so that we do not lose collective memory.

> — Frederick R. Karl, author of ***Joseph Conrad: The Three Lives. A Biography***, ***William Faulkner: American Writer. A Biography***, and ***Franz Kafka: Representative Man. A Biography***

These magnificent poems are an assault on our complacency, our sleeping memories. Every line of *Gestapo Crows*, wrenched from a stricken heart, reminds us that each of us died in the ovens of the holocaust, that the crimes of the Nazi era were crimes against our humanity, too, and that all of us have a moral obligation to *remember*. Mr. Brodsky's poetic voice, now sadly meditative, now a cry from the ashes, is a haunting, anguished triumph of memory over evil.

— Stephen B. Oates, author of the Christopher Award-winning *With Malice Toward None: The Life of Abraham Lincoln* and the Robert F. Kennedy Memorial Book Award-winning *Let the Trumpet Sound: The Life of Martin Luther King, Jr.*

The Holocaust represented the triumph of evil over good. Again, Louis Daniel Brodsky touches our very being with awesome poetic reminders. He brilliantly stirs our hearts and strengthens our resolve that good may yet triumph over evil. His poetry remains not just as words to be read, but as history which must be studied.

— Alvan D. Rubin, Rabbi Emeritus, Temple Israel, St. Louis, Missouri

To the immense and ever-growing library of Holocaust books must be added Louis Daniel Brodsky's *Gestapo Crows*. Almost unbearably graphic — how can it be otherwise? — and yet imaginative, outraged and remarkably personal, these poems exemplify the contagion of the horror which more than any other series of events, mars the name of the Twentieth Century.

— Karl Shapiro, author of *Poems of a Jew*, *The Bourgeois Poet*, and the Pulitzer Prize-winning *V-Letter and Other Poems*

Reading *Gestapo Crows*, I was transported back in time to the discourses of the Hebrew prophet Hosea. Hosea's faithless wife is a metaphor for the faithlessness of Biblical Israel. Her adultery is the adultery of a nation whoring after foreign gods who cannot redeem Israel from destruction. Louis Brodsky turns the metaphor upside down and blows the reader away. First, Brodsky defines in stark and powerful language his total immersion and identification with the pain of the Holocaust from the perspective of an American Jew. Then, using the sacred language of the Holocaust, the greatest tragedy to befall any people, he performs what must have been a painful autopsy on his own failed marriage. Is this misuse of the Holocaust? Not if it compels the reader to evaluate all actions and relationships in terms of their life-destructive potential. The power of the Holocaust to teach us lessons of human understanding must not be limited to history and political science. Brodsky's *Gestapo Crows* is a daring effort, not easily ignored. It is not poetry for the faint of heart.

— Rabbi Mark L. Shook, Senior Rabbi, Temple Israel, St. Louis, Missouri

In the Holocaust the history of a generation of Jews became an exemplification of what seems to be a necessary motive in human history: the recurrent need of men to do primordial violence to each other. In this case the fact that the act of violence was unprecedented in extent and ferocity has not essentially transformed the historical motive of the second generation of survivors, those born "too late to really remember but not late enough to forget the Nazi atrocities of World War II." Encountering the need to survive their own, the post-Holocaust, history — the ironic, subtle, pervasive need to save themselves from a destructive obsession with revenge of the dead — they have, for the sake of having their own history, largely surrendered, as second generation survivors always do, to the alienation of memory by history. Typically it has been bardic poets who have countered the alienation of memory by assuming the holy mission of serving remembrance. Ironically in Louis Daniel Brodsky's *Gestapo Crows*, we discover an American Jewish poet who believes himself to be uniquely charged with fierce and absolute resistance to the surrender of memory by second-generation American Jews, but who speaks finally — especially in his climactic recording of the tragedy of the marriage of a gentile and a committed Jew — not in a bardic but in a haunted and compelling lyrical voice. Although the analogy is limited, one may say in his poems that Brodsky, a devoted student of William Faulkner, who also spoke basically in a lyrical voice, has created an American Jewish Gothic that, like Faulkner's Southern Gothic, is capable of expressing a vision of history at once absurd and extraordinarily powerful.

> — Lewis P. Simpson, Consulting Editor of *The Southern Review* and author of *The Dispossessed Garden: Pastoral and History in Southern Literature*

In some magical way L.D. Brodsky has managed to short-circuit the readers' normal sensory input. The rhythms of his poetry are the beat of our hearts, his narrative drive the flow of our blood, his powerful imagery our own sinew and bone. When we read *Gestapo Crows* we are, regardless of our heritage, Jews, our essence comingled with the ashes of our brethren, each of us shouting our silent rage.

> — Robert Vaughan, author of *The American Chronicles*

One cannot but respond with deep emotion and affection to the anguish and pain one finds in your poems. Granted, words are often unable to express the ineffable; but isn't poetry the art of transcending words?

> — Elie Wiesel, winner of the 1986 Nobel Peace Prize and author of *Night*

GESTAPO CROWS
HOLOCAUST POEMS

Books by
LOUIS DANIEL BRODSKY

Poetry

Trilogy: A Birth Cycle (1974)
Monday's Child (1975)
The Kingdom of Gewgaw (1976)
Point of Americas II (1976)
Preparing for Incarnations (1976)
La Preciosa (1977)
Stranded in the Land of Transients (1978)
The Uncelebrated Ceremony of Pants Factory Fatso (1978)
Birds in Passage (1980)
Résumé of a Scrapegoat (1980)
Mississippi Vistas: Volume One of *A Mississippi Trilogy* (1983) (1990)
You Can't Go Back, Exactly (1988)
The Thorough Earth (1989)
Four and Twenty Blackbirds Soaring (1989)
Falling from Heaven: Holocaust Poems of a Jew and a Gentile
   (with William Heyen) (1991)
Forever, for Now: Poems for a Later Love   (1991)
Mistress Mississippi: Volume Three of *A Mississippi Trilogy*   (1992)
A Gleam in the Eye: Poems for a First Baby   (1992)
Gestapo Crows: Holocaust Poems   (1992)

Bibliography (Coedited with Robert Hamblin)

Selections from the William Faulkner Collection of Louis Daniel Brodsky:
   A Descriptive Catalogue (1979)
Faulkner: A Comprehensive Guide to the Brodsky Collection
      Volume I: The Biobibliography (1982)
      Volume II: The Letters (1984)
      Volume III: The De Gaulle Story (1984)
      Volume IV: Battle Cry (1985)
      Volume V: Manuscripts and Documents (1989)
*Country Lawye*r and Other Stories for the Screen by William
   Faulkner   (1987)
Stallion Road: A Screenplay by William Faulkner (1989)

Biography

William Faulkner, Life Glimpses (1990)

GESTAPO CROWS
HOLOCAUST POEMS

by Louis Daniel Brodsky

Louis Daniel Brodsky

12/30/07

St. Louis, MO

TIME BEING BOOKS
POETRY IN SIGHT AND SOUND
Saint Louis, Missouri

Time Being Books
10411 Clayton Road
Saint Louis, Missouri 63131

Time Being Books volumes are printed on acid-free paper, and binding
materials are chosen for strength and durability.

ISBN 1-877770-76-0
ISBN 1-877770-77-9 (pbk.)
ISBN 1-877770-78-7 (tape)

Library of Congress Cataloging-in-Publication Data

Brodsky, Louis Daniel.
    Gestapo crows: Holocaust poems / by Louis Daniel Brodsky. —
1st ed.
        p.   cm.
        ISBN 1-877770-76-0 (alk. paper): $16.95. —ISBN 1-877770-77-9
(pbk. : alk. paper) : $9.95
        1. Holocaust, Jewish (1939-1945)—Poetry. 2. Holocaust survi-
vors—Poetry. 3. Jews—Poetry. I. Title.
PS3552.R623G47   1992
811'.54—dc20   92-60745
                                                            CIP

Manufactured in the United States of America

First Edition, first printing (November 1992)

Acknowledgments

For their rigorous collaboration with me in revising this book, I am indebted to Time Being Books' dedicated staff: Jane Goldberg, Editor in Chief, who privileges my poems with her wisdom and insight; Jerry Call, Senior Editor, whose keen ear helps keep my cadences balanced and contributes to the clarity of my diction; Sheri Vandermolen, Editor and Archivist, whose persistent scrutiny of my syntax and the mechanics of language enhances my verse; and Lori Loesche, Assistant Editor, who, in addition to reading copy, was responsible for typesetting this manuscript.

My thanks go to Ruth Dambach, who has provided her technical expertise in overseeing the composition and design of this book; her good taste is formidable.

I am grateful to the Levitt Foundation for permission to reproduce Mauricio Lasansky's *Nazi Drawing* #23 as the illustration for the cover of this book. I am especially appreciative of Professor Lasansky for making a rare exception in consenting to allow one of his masterful drawings to be seen out of the context of the complete *Nazi Drawings*.

I also extend my appreciation to the editors of the *St. Louis Jewish Light*, in which earlier versions of the following poems appeared: "My Holocaust Flowers," "Grodsky the Cobbler," "The Forest," and "Tending the Flock."

I acknowledge Faber and Faber, Inc. Publisher for permission to reprint "The Crow's Song," from *Collected Poems*, by Primo Levi, English translation copyright © 1988 by Ruth Feldman and Brian Swann; to Doubleday, a division of Bantam Doubleday Dell Publishing Group, Inc., for permission to reprint "Night Crow," from *The Collected Poems of Theodore Roethke*, by Theodore Roethke, copyright © 1944 by Saturday Review Association, Inc.; and to HarperCollins for permission to reprint an excerpt from Sylvia Plath's "Mary's Song," from *The Collected Poems of Sylvia Plath*, edited by Ted Hughes, copyright © 1963 by Ted Hughes.

To you,

who have picked up *Gestapo Crows*
out of moral responsibility,
guilt,
or curiosity
and possess the fortitude and courage
to stick with your intuition
to read it,

I dedicate this book.

'I came from very far away
To bring bad news.
I flew across the mountain,
Pierced the low cloud,
Mirrored my belly in the pond.
I flew without resting,
A hundred miles without resting,
To find your window,
To find your ear,
To bring you the sad tidings
That rob you of sleep's joy,
That taint your bread and wine,
Lodge every evening in your heart.'
    This is the way he sang, dancing, vicious,
    Beyond the glass, upon the snow.
    As he fell silent, he looked about, malign,
    Marked a cross on the ground with his beak,
    And opened his black wings wide.

"The Crow's Song"
— Primo Levi

When I saw that clumsy crow
Flap from a wasted tree,
A shape in the mind rose up:
Over the gulfs of dream
Flew a tremendous bird
Further and further away
Into a moonless black,
Deep in the brain, far back.

"Night Crow"
— Theodore Roethke

Gray birds obsess my heart,
Mouth-ash, ash of eye.
They settle. On the high

Precipice
That emptied one man into space
The ovens glowed like heavens, incandescent.

It is a heart,
This holocaust I walk in,
O golden child the world will kill and eat.

from "Mary's Song"
— Sylvia Plath

Contents

Prologue

GESTAPO CROWS
HOLOCAUST POEMS

* This symbol has been used to indicate that a stanza has been broken due to pagination.

Prologue

The Evolution of Man

In his most graphic dreams,
He encounters a recurring theme:
Violence.
His sleep is besieged with screaming silence
Issuing from myriad precursors of modern man —
Australopithecus
And *Homo sapiens*, Neanderthal and Cro-Magnon —
Executing grotesque acts of homicide
By ripping invaders *and* tribesmen
Limb from hirsute limb
And viciously dismembering fingers, toes,
Heads, testicles, and breasts
With premeditated, sadistic bestiality.

In this cave-pocked desolation,
Creatured by these genocidal beasts
Systematically cannibalizing their own species,
Carnivores of the basest kind,
He recognizes sinister signs of malignance
Infiltrating the existing order.
He spies a pictograph,
Certainly informed by a higher intellect,
Scraped across the face of a limestone cliff,
Consisting of two intersecting lines,
One end of each thrusting left, the other right:
A swastika,
Not yet assigned its place in the evolution of Man.

CHAPTER ONE

FIRESTORM —
VICTIMS

Franz, Prague, 1919

For Frederick R. Karl

His ears are always buzzing with fears:
Wasps hovering around their nest,
In and out, out and in
And out, again and again.

He is insectile, stifled by his own voice
Screaming in dark mazes
Pleas of innocence against imaginary crimes:
Patricide, child molestation, blood libel,

Masturbatory celibacy, and anomie.
He weeps at his helplessness
In defending himself against charges
Made in the State's appellate courts

And sentences imposed by apprentices,
Law students actually,
Doing their internships on human guinea pigs
Brought before the Grand Inquisitor to be taunted;

He's frightened by his own rage,
A screeching gibbon in a zoo cage
Being gawked at by well-paid Peeping Toms
Who hope to locate a crucial clue

To his undisclosed identity — a tic,
Word-slur, Freudian slip of the flicking tongue,
Or other parapraxis —
By which they might psychoanalyze him

Without jeopardizing their precious reputations.
He exists in constant trepidation,
Nightmaring scenarios in which he's arrested,
One fine morning, by two Cyclopes,

Traduced (whatever, he's not yet determined,
This specific, disturbing verb means),
And trundled off to an internment camp
To lose his freedom forever.

Although he's never been late
Making his insurance appraisals, processing claims,
Never been reproached for breaches of protocol,
Like being absent or eating at his work station,

He lives from year to year with phobias
And subliminal cultural guilt,
Fabricated yet as real as the holocaust he envisions
Waking and asleep. Being a marginal man,

Closet writer with a subversive bite,
Superfluous Jew, he just might decide tonight
To metamorphose into a tubercular bug
And die on his back from dehydration, not fire.

First Violinist Israelievitch, Berlin, 1933

Sitting on his front stoop,
Hearing twilight's sibilances multiply
Like ripples from a stone thrown into an ocean,
He recognizes leitmotifs
Floating on the breeze
And begins to score lyrical glissandi
Neither melodic nor cacophonous
But hypnotically beguiling;
Even the crickets stop their monotony
While he tunes his instrument to divinity's pitch
In the key of Infinity.

But the deeper he concentrates,
The more intuitively he perceives leaves
Twisting as they fall through the distant darkness
Into the Abyss against whose edge he presses.
He resists listening, peering into the crater,
For fear he might experience his own disappearance.
Instead, he transposes their brittle frictions
By bowing the sky's violin strings
Into an intricate motet
Composed of deathless Deathnotes
He hopes to sing next spring.

Hyman Weiss, Court Reporter, Düsseldorf, 1935

This April morning,
Disoriented by the four-day workweek
Celebrating the Führer's birthday,
He hastily downs three cups of coffee
Before heading to the Ministry
To resume operating his stenograph,
Recording testimony from witnesses
Opposing lawyers have been questioning all week:
The petty, sleazy stuff of infidelity
He registers stoically
As though life's unfolding soap-opera script
Were a sequel to God's Covenant etched on stone,
Dead Sea Scrolls
He reproduces daily
On a continuous, three-inch-wide roll of paper.

Chancing to glance at the watch
That constricts his arthritic wrist
(He blames this on aging
Rather than on the 200-word-per-minute speed
His fingers average nine hours a day),
He realizes he's remained at the *Kaffee Haus*
A half-hour later than normal
And that by now the legal proceedings have begun
Without his services or been postponed —
Either way, this sole lapse won't go unrecorded
By those who depend on his reliability.
In truth, he fears his miscue will be used in Court
When his superiors bring suits against him
For negligence, ineptitude,
And alleged, though not yet proven, Jewishness.

Foregone Delusions, Germany, 1937

People who live in glass caskets
Shouldn't throw bones,
Not even their own,
Unless they expect to be found hiding alone,
Above ground,
As though fulfilling a cultural decree:
Mass sacrificial sepulture.

Day after day, eulogies permeate the air
With choking putrescence;
The stench fuses all hues into one:
Carcinogenic black.
The earth grows top-heavy,
Lopsided with skeletal accretion,
Wobbles awry, begins to drift, splinter,

But then a godly force field
Reenergizes its hold,
Locking the planet into orbit at the last moment
Before Apocalypse succeeds
In annihilating man's dreams for immortality;
Meanwhile, the drowsy populace
Repeats its prayers, preparing for Sleep.

The Gathering Storm, Europe, 1938

All the baleful day,
A black, tattered wind has changed directions;
Now, assuming the guise of a demonic banshee,
It screams down a blistered sky,
A psychotic patient
Breaking constraints, escaping his cell,
A Doberman, teeth bared, foaming at the gums,
Biting blindly at telephone poles,
Trolleys, signposts, people,
Finally chewing itself into extinction
Without dying.

Afternoon accedes, by degrees, to night's force:
The wide, lightning-riddled sky
Is a Krupp-muzzle,
An erupting volcano's crater
Seen from the earth's core,
A cosmic chimney whose ashen debris
Pocks eyeglasses, watch crystals,
Store, home, and factory windows,
And nickel-plated car parts
Before scratching scabs off festering wounds.
Quiescent bones, moldering six feet below,

Grow restive as though the rabid Universe
Were bent on retribution
And, at any moment, might call for all monies
Owed for investments bought on margin
In Death's short-term, terrestrial offering.
But the inevitable Apocalypse stalls,
Defuses its ultimate threat,
Somehow suppresses its horrific, pestilent fury
(Doubtless for a later occasion)
While each of us,
Professing his ignorant innocence

And yet assessing his own potential for selfishness,
Petty human cruelty, and destruction
In nature's cessation,
Proceeds to annihilate every blessed dream
Mankind might have hoped to achieve.
Absolved from responsibility for final solutions
And believing that the diabolical wind
Is all hot air,
We go to bed intoxicated,
Sharing Chamberlain's Munich Pact delusion
Of "peace for our time."

Firestorm, Germany, 1939

Today he takes off hastily
To make rounds through his foundering Kingdom,
Distressed, anxious to assess the damage
Inflicted by hooligans and Brownshirts
During his people's most recent *Kristallnacht*.

Abruptly uprooted from the leisurely breakfast
He's grown used to eating
Throughout his years of assimilation,
He primes himself to witness the ravagement
He suspects he'll find in his city-states,

Whose fortifications he's allowed to deteriorate
Not from laziness so much as complacence,
Which has deluded him
Into believing himself immune to disease,
Self-righteousness, even greed,

Qualities he's assumed unwittingly
Through emulation of those controlling souls
Who over the years have accepted him,
Albeit with a xenophobia
Disguised as tolerance of *Volksjuden*.

The glaring *Autobahn* he drives too fast
This last day of the first month of a year
He doesn't yet realize will mark his final *Aktion*
Blinds him as the sun's invasive rays
Refract into his dazed eyes.

Somewhere in the distance that could be noon
Or yesteryear or the tomorrow
He can't possibly know will be his burial day,
He sees eerie tornados of purple smoke
Violently spiraling toward his speeding vehicle,

Rings hovering in the vicinity of the Kingdom
He's considered his hideaway — Faith —
That sacred, secluded estate
To which, he assured himself, he could always retreat
If ever he needed to flee his beloved *Vaterland*.

Degenerate Poet, Heidelberg, 1940

He has no idea just how or when
The spore attached itself to his brain,
That core where logic and metaphor fuse
To form the creative cognition
That keeps him sane in a hostile environment
Controlled by Germ-anic bacteria
Conspiring with Gestapo viruses
To scourge dreams and Dead Sea Scrolls
Just by encouraging him to assimilate,
Remain opaque to blatant racists,
Lupine politicos in sheep's clothing,
And pseudointellectuals in cafés,
Who, gaining his confidence,
Would impale his kike-head on a pike

And parade it through their city-states
To keep riotous natives satisfied
Long enough to complete their coup d'état
And assume centralized power
Before devouring them *and* each other
At ubiquitous Wannsee Conferences
Convened to enact any modest proposals
Their Commander in Chief might conceive,
Including isolation, then genocide,
His lasting contribution to mankind.
At all costs, almost, at least until now,
He's maintained his disguise of lowly poet,
Impecunious, posing no sub-verse-ive threat
To the corrosive status quo.

But lately, poems he's surreptitiously penned
In his moldy basement,
Poems construable as seditious
By censors at the Ministry of Propaganda,
Poems whose between-the-lines subtexts
Of subliminal messages
Recite biting indictments against the State
With calls to oust the Nazis
*

And reinstate those who cherish freedom of speech,
Tolerate dissent, advocate the vote,
Poems inadvertently circulated,
Have come under the scrutiny of Dr. Mengele,
Who's determined that he's contracted a disease
Requiring surgical extermination: Judaism.

Kafkaesque Vestiges, Germany, 1941

The hours have needlelike teeth
And ravenous scavenger appetites;
They spy rotting flesh the Director leaves behind
And, like cannibals eating their own raw meat,
Suck dry the marrow and greasy juices
Oozing from oven-opened pores,
Devour it live.
Soon Time will consume
Integuments of Memory and muscle,
Then drain entire tributaries of blood
From Civilization's alluvial basin
Into its own Dead Sea
Before it drips down the Abyss,
Depositing along its brain-cave's ceiling
And grave's floor
Broken, rusty stalactites and stalagmites
Similar to those used
In Germany's penal-colony machines.

Although he can't predict Fate's fickleness
Or History's inconstancy,
Those perfidious mistresses of Pharaohs and Führers,
At this late hour
He should be able to guess the grisly outcome
Of this Director of Jewish Destiny,
This self-anointed,
Messianic killer of Christ Killers,
Savior of the pure of heart, the true Teutonic:
Ultimately he'll come atumble too,
Falling into his erratic contraption,
His naked body emptying its blue-red fluids
Through perforations in his face, chest,
Abdomen, groin, and anus,
Which, when scabbed over, will create a tattoo
Forming a "*J*" for *Jude* for all to see
Who may meet his spectral shade
Vaporizing forever in Valhalla's nether regions.

Under the Circumstances,
Warsaw Ghetto, 1942

Surviving in the ghetto
Has its occasional consolations,
Its brief reprieves,
But they're not always easy to detect
When the cock crows with a loon's hysteria,
The stork refuses to transport cargo,
And the cuckoo ululates its idiotic ritual
Every hour, dark and light,
Intimating the Gestapo's imminent knock at the door.

Although the insomnious waiting is torture,
Horror does exempt us
From tending to chores, maintaining decorum;
No one expends much energy anymore
Lamenting each recent surrender to Death.
We've even suspended teaching, praying,
Meeting collectively to discuss events
We've absolutely no say-so in swaying;
Resignation is easier to sustain than faith.

More to the point: who would have ever believed
We'd condone, let alone encourage,
Our own women to solicit on street corners
Where our patricians once convened
Or that we would become History's pimps,
Forcing our wives and daughters
To lie down on their backs, spread their legs,
And make the gates of their temples
Accessible to *anyone* with pfennigs for bread?

Valediction Forbidding Despair, Cracow Ghetto, 1943

This summer is Treblinka;
Its regimental months are ovens that arrest us
In bloodless custody,
Dress us in evaporating memory-ashes.
Victims, like crickets
Scratching dryness from limbs,
Chant hymns through lips that shape the air
With unfinished kisses;
We listen with bleeding disbelief,
Knowing soon we'll meet in *Gan Eden*.

Musicians, carpenters, midwives, physicians,
Zionists and assimilationists
Yet amidst us
Guard the darker silences
Of those who crowd naked each day
Into boxcars and chambers,
Where almond-perfumed night descends.
Premonitions race down chutes
To steaming graves
Time spreads with quicklime and fertilizer.

But the spirit exists outside ideologies,
Or it should, anyway;
The end obliterates nothing, really,
Except flesh
And the evanescent death wish
To rest just long enough
To catch one's breath
Before resuming the necessary trek
Toward Memory's ultimate destination,
Resurrection.

CHAPTER TWO

SMOLDERING ASHES —
REFUGEES

The Ice Age

This crisp, glistening December morning,
As he drives away from the City,
His eyes rise
Through thousands of chimney flues
Spewing innocuous plumes of gas-furnace heat
That condenses to white smoke on hitting the air.
He imagines myriad anonymous spirits
Going about their routine business
Of wiping Sleep's hallucinations from their eyes
And slipping into necessary disguises
As they cake fresh makeup over old layers
Or stretch facial masks into place
Before donning sheep costumes appropriate to jobs
Each performs with soulless zealotry.

He sees them, the entire herd,
Languishing in a collective shower,
Dressing, then driving in their cattle cars
To work on Death's assembly lines
Fabricating ashes designed by inhuman beings
For human ghosts to use throughout their lives
Floating from limbo to Limbo
Below God's boneyard between firmament and Eternity.
That he's been gifted with these powers of insight
Doesn't make him privileged, just chosen;
He'd sacrifice anything but his faith
To drive by winter-bound houses like these
Without remembering Lodz Ghetto and Auschwitz,
Which he almost escaped fifty ice ages ago.

Leah

Approaching his seventieth year,
He notices his nightly routine veering
With increasing predictability
From watching sitcoms and movies on TV
To sitting by himself
In the kitchen, his *locus mundus*,
Where he microwaves frozen meals
And stares vacantly
Until sleep inundates his tired eyes.
He can't assess what's possessed him lately,
Yet, for days (maybe weeks or months),
He's been fantasizing about his wife, Leah,
As he did in the Warsaw Ghetto in '43

During that hiatus between her deportation
And the perilous escape he made
From his putative *Vaterland*,
When he couldn't suppress that grotesque after-image
Those Brownshirted Gestapo crows
Etched on his retinas
As they dragged her by the hair,
Naked, wrested from their lovemaking,
Down two flights of stairs
To a snorting transport train
At the *Umschlagplatz*, three blocks away.
Curiously, he's been seized
Not with memories but libidinous urges for her,

Real, erotic feelings: blood-rushes,
Erections without obvious provocation,
And what, in youth, they called "wet dreams"
And "lover's nuts." It's so crazy!
Especially for one as abstemious as he,
Who, for almost half a century,
Has ascetically repressed all sexual thoughts
Out of respect for her blessed soul.
But if, once again,
He's craving sensual pleasure,
Then he'll continue masturbating
Whenever she appears to him —
Biblical sin or not.

Smoldering Ashes

For the last three nights,
His dreams have been ravaged by demons,
Chimeras, amorphous amebas,
And galactic arachnids
Rappelling from Piranesian chains
Onto his sweat-soaked bed,
Bolted to the trapdoor
Above the Abyss Satan named Babi Yar,
Then willed into nonexistence,
Charging his Field Marshal, Schicklgruber,
With using only human landfill and Time-lime
To insure its invisibility to History —
A nearly impossible trick
Even for the Prince of Darkness himself!

Each night under the covers,
He's twisted and lunged,
Shredded his shroud-sheets,
Screamed, hissed, snarled,
And plunged over bed's edge
As if leaping from a flaming, listing ship
Into an ocean of Jewish bones.
Never certain whether awake
Or swimming on the surface of infernal Nightmare,
He submits to the gaseous stench,
The horrific, silent Gorgon-roaring
Of those chosen souls
Emanating from the trench over which he swings
Each time Dream's executioner trips the trapdoor.

O, if only he could commit his soul to the Deep,
Experience corruption with all those others
Who've known the intimacy
Of sleeping in communal nakedness.
But this unexpungeable punishment
Is too much to endure.
O, the irony of having survived that firestorm
To be visited nightly
By the devilish specter of Hitler,
*

Who, pitchforking their fired bones,
Keeps his own smoldering ashes aglow.
O, if only he could unscrew the bolts gyving his bed,
He might loosen Hallucination's hold on Memory
And dream the dreams angels in *Gan Eden* dream.

Meeting His Own Shadow Coming and Going

Fleeing southwesterly
Down Highway 55 toward Festus,
He sneezes three times;
"It's the season," he reasonably concedes
While viewing across the median
A segmented snake slithering from side to side,
A reptile with glistening scales,
Its headlights outshining the sun's crisp radiance,
A cortège led by a black Cadillac hearse,
Death itself on a tear
This otherwise innocuous afternoon.

Almost never surprised
By his ability to metaphorize even the mundane,
He nonetheless contemplates the odds
Of ever again sneezing three times
As a corpse snakes its way to the graveyard;
Then, immediately, he proceeds to dismiss,
As merely coincidental, this concurrence,
A perfectly gratuitous miscue
In Fate's timetable. Yet, he grows apprehensive
Approaching the apex of a steep grade
As he sees a gray smolder

Billowing from what appears to be a deep ravine;
The smoke is a snake
Slithering side to side into the blue sky.
As he draws closer, the chasm widens,
Summons him to its uneven edges.
He pulls onto the shoulder,
Peers fearfully into a primordial necropolis
Crammed with fired skeletons.
Suddenly he begins to sneeze from the thick odors,
Realizing he's just passed his own hearse
Heading home, empty.

Gestapo Crow

Each refugee a.m.,
When Sam Deutschlander awakens,
Completely naked, penis limp
Despite having to urinate fiercely,
Shivering, teeth chattering winter and summer,
Throws off his bedsheets,
And stands at attention on the balls of his feet
As Memory rigidly suspends him
In antic salute
For seconds that exhume him from the depths of decades,
He realizes his two-legged, hand-wound,
Radium-illuminated,
Chromeplated alarm clock
Is a Gestapo crow
Whose spastic clapper, slapping its two shrieking bells,
Is a beak pecking his brain lobes,
Forcing him each morning, punctually,
To awaken from the dead, eschew suicide, and flee.

Crimes Against Humanity

This inordinately early morning,
An argentiferous mist
Lifts between sky and trees,
Enfencing his eyes' tormented horizon.
He has no idea why he's driving south
Unless it's to elude Sleep's neo-Nazis,
Stalking alleys and side streets
Of the ghetto from which he's perpetually retreating —
He had not one extra second
To grab possessions
During their *Blitzkrieg* last night-mare
Or to act upon his Wiesenthal dreams.

Conceivably he's being too dramatic,
Stating the case with ironic hyperbole;
Probably this ominous mist, now crimson,
Portends nothing less nor more
Than the severe thunderstorm
His radio's been forecasting repeatedly
These past three hours.
Yet perhaps he's actually fled this time,
Not to elude Nazis
But to hunt down his fugitive hallucination,
Extradite and punish it
For crimes against his humanity.

Train Trips to Auschwitz and All Points West

This quiet Saturday sunrise,
His ears fail to recognize vectoring echoes
Homing in on this planet;
They can't distinguish his lips' whispers
From introspective intellections
Screaming across synapses like passenger trains
Tearing between small-town crossing gates.
In one sense, he can confirm his vegetable existence
(His tongue and throat know he's sipping coffee
Though they've no idea
His location is *this* café near the motel
His loneliness rents by the day),
Yet in another, seated here by himself,
He may even be dead or dying.

Worse, his synaptic apparatus may be short-circuiting.
In truth, those spectral trains,
Instead of transporting ordinary commuters
East to west, may be hauling *Sonderzüge*
To Nazi meat-packing plants
Or *Wehrmacht* ammunition factories,
Their sinister destinations those grotesque depots
Rising like Leviathans,
Their primordial jaws opened wide
To sift Germanic and Polish oceans
For human diatoms and plankton
That drift unwittingly into their maws
To be turned into fecal matter,
Food-chain fuel to sustain future generations.

Either way, the Reich-*Bahnnetz* runs on time,
Forcing his psyche to draft the architecture
Of a colossal, empty *Umschlagplatz*
His dreams rebuild each evening
To receive the freights deporting his amnesic spirit
From Nightmare to the distant Abyss.
Nothing he takes relieves his insomnia:
Trains rumbling through his brain's terrain
*

Leave in their ceaseless wakes
Cinders, ash, dead air, white silence,
Creating an *Endlösung* so terrible
All his thoughts, like this morning's, go deaf
Striving to survive who he was, is,
And must necessarily become.

Celebrating Independence Day

Sitting on the porch by himself
This holiday morning,
Listening, not quite absentmindedly,
To birdsongs, whirring lawn mowers,
And the sporadic roars of jets taking off
From the airport ten miles away,
He can neither deny nor sidetrack anxieties
That have shadowed him systematically
These past forty-five years,
Traced him all this distance through history
To this solitary place in space and time.

Even on this absolutely innocuous "*Volksfest*,"
The masses' nationally declared "Sabbath,"
He regards squirrels and birds suspiciously,
As though they might be Trojan Horses
With hollow bellies waiting to release,
Through trapdoors, Gestapo agents
Whose orders would unloose *SS* Storm Troops
To infiltrate his yard, the park, City Hall,
The entire country in a "Lightning War"
Without the slightest resistance
From bewildered, intimidated citizens like himself.

Although he's experienced a degree of security,
Contentment has been a provisional element
In the equation whose elusive "x"
Keeps fluxing from factor to product,
Right side to left;
Sleeping and being awake, the two knowns,
Have frustrated him with restless questioning
As to the interpretation of nightmares,
The meaning of jettisoned dreams and visions,
Prophecies, hallucinations, and omens
Like the one that demonized him last evening:

Resisting the air conditioner's relief,
Despite ninety-degree heat at eleven,
For fear of going stiff in his muscles and joints,
He pushed the sheets off his back.
While sneaking up on sleep,
He must have initiated their plunge,
His feet lightly nudging them
Over bed's edge, down the abyss into a pit,
Like dead bodies. Before they hit bottom,
A vagrant premonition awakened him
To the apparition of his own clammy, naked body.

Sweating and nauseous, resting on bony haunches,
With an ineffectual erection throbbing between his legs,
As if awaiting detumescence
To let him withdraw it from Death's anus,
He couldn't assess his location at first,
Not until his eyes spied the sign
Above the door to his own bedroom,
ARBEIT MACHT FREI,*
And he realized he'd died again in his sleep.
Now, sitting outdoors this Fourth of July,
He ponders the irony of it all.

* Sign over the entrance gate that greeted all new deportees to
Auschwitz death camp: WORK MAKES ONE FREE.

The Book Burner

"When books are burned,
people are burned."
— Heinrich Heine

Yesterday afternoon,
At loose ends and without suitable alternatives
To relax his all-too-diffuse mind,
He decided to spend a few idle hours
Browsing through antique shops and used-book stores
In downtown St. Louis.
Scanning the precisely categorized titles
Swelling the shelves
Of Wagner's World-Wide Editions,
He noticed a sign on a case
Labeled WW II,
"Inquire at desk for Nazi materials,"
And, as if grasping a croker sack of hissing cobras
He knew better than to open,
Approached the owner to make his request.

Like a hibernating bear
Waking from millennial slumber
Or a nightmare exploding to the surface
Of this cave-dwelling seller's psyche,
The ghost of Gustav Wagner
Rose from his overstuffed sofa behind the register,
Disappeared into an opaque corridor,
His sanctum sanctorum,
And lumbered to the counter with a packet of pamphlets,
Each printed in cryptic, black-and-red,
Gothic calligraphy,
Some in English, some in German,
All dated, on the verso of the title page
Or at the foot of the back cover,
1938.

One title arrested and exterminated his thoughts
As though state agents had caught them
Breaking into the Ministry of Propaganda,
Where the Gestapo kept its documents
On perverts, Gypsies, idiots,
Syphilitics, malcontents, homosexuals,
And Christ-killing race defilers:
What to Do About the Jewish Question.
Petrified, he flipped through its brittle pages,
Felt himself grow nauseated.
Frantically, one fist clutching the sinister booklet,
He ran from the store into the street
And, unconscious of his *Aktion*,
Heaved it into the sun's sputtering ash heap,
Not even stopping to watch it ignite.

Playing Ostrich

During the nearly two decades
He's spent in this Midwestern oasis
Since arriving from Vienna via Buenos Aires,
He hasn't attended synagogue
As if to do so, even in St. Louis,
Might jeopardize his existence;
In fact, to this day,
He's not taken a trolley,
Driven a Volkswagen or Mercedes-Benz,
Nor even considered purchasing a Leica or Rolleiflex
Despite his passion for photographing farmhouses,
Old factories, birds in passage,
And children, in parks and on schoolgrounds,
Lost in innocent distractions.
But this year he's debating celebrating Rosh Hashanah.

For twenty years, forever,
He's played the proverbial ostrich
(Or so he's thought)
By trying to remove from his will to live
His ineradicable Yiddish dialect,
Unstraightenable curls, and hooked nose —
Hoping to disown those Semitic features
That so blatantly marked him as a pariah
In his European avatar —
And by legally changing his name
From Abe Abramowitz to Ray Bramley
In order to melt into mainstream America
Without a trace of his ungainly shadow
Following in obsessive lockstep,
Mocking him as it did in the unspeakable days;

The shadow remarkably similar
To that pterodactylic, two-headed predator
His motherland, Österreich,
Adopted as its symbol of nationalistic pride
To adorn postage stamps,
Official bulletins, and civic buildings
*

As well as to tattoo the psyches
Of an all-too-obedient and believing people
Completely suited to the Hitlerian mentality
That had risen in the 1890s
From its Viennese phoenix-nest
Just in time to save Austria from racial ruination,
That monstrous image, to this day so tenacious
That playing Österreich
Seems a cruelly ironic contradiction in terms.

Lately, he's been feeling an emptiness
He can't remember suffering since fleeing
In September of 1939,
After the occupation and Nazification occurred,
And now, with tomorrow evening's start
Of the Jewish New Year,
He senses an unnameable agent or *Geist*
Compelling him to come out of hiding,
Proclaim his opaque presence
To this tiny minority of privileged misfits,
Who've chosen to make St. Louis their "homeland,"
By attending synagogue with them,
Honoring those once-sacred rituals,
And chanting prayers he recited as a child in Wien
Before burying his head in the sands of Time.

Revisiting Childhood Haunts

This day is a series of blunt, geometric shadows
    cast from shapes in a Sheeler factory scape.
As he drives further away from the City,
    vision's cataracts lose their opacity,
And the past emerges with teary familiarity
    as he sees a wooded estate, like the one in Bremen,
Where his Youth attained manhood
    within white-columned splendors of Innocence.

Suddenly, a hundred crows, like chunks of coal
    strewn along a railroad track,
Interrupt his reverie, blacken the atmosphere,
    fill the air with a plague of locusts;
His pupils dilate in darkening despair,
    fearing for their very existence;
Talons and beaks scratch the afternoon sky
    with crosshatched images of doom.

His eyes search in every direction
    for carrion or fresh flesh
Left to November for immediate disposal.
    No recognizable miasmas lift
From the furious, cawing congestion of birds,
    yet, in a flash, his retinas detect
Effigies of deathly dimension.
    His shouts are rocks hurled at a pool's surface;

The crows scatter, their shattering cacophony
    splintering the infant world's crust into space
As they dissolve from sight.
    He enters an unsurmised Forest behind his eyes
Where, despite his absence all these years,
    nightmares from childhood survive,
Then he follows the crows to its core, his future,
    to see if he still exists.

Lost in a Crowd, 1990

Tripping through grooming rituals
This Wednesday morning after Labor Day,
He splashes arsenic-hued toothpaste on the mirror,
Nicks his chin with a dull razor blade,
Forgets to collect ghost-hair from his comb
And thumb it into the latrine,
Then reaches for a vitamin from his depleted supply.
Last night's dead sleep,
Back and forth to the earth's core,
Might have been forty-nine years deep
For the malaise that seems to have surfaced within him.

Just now, staring at his ashen body,
He sees a dazed stranger
(Whether hobo loping along a train track
Or shell-shocked soldier navigating bomb craters
In a desolate landscape, he can't differentiate)
Scrutinizing him through flaming eyes
That might be set in the head of a predatory leopard
Or cobra instead of his own face;
He winces, twitches, shakes
As if defibrillator paddles
Were riveted to his chest, jolting his heart.

Even after chugging three cups of coffee,
He remains too composed for his phantasmagoria
To be detected by colleagues and enemies
Who would abuse his compliance.
He'll conceal his unhealed feelings with aplomb;
No one will realize he's numb from ear to ear,
Head to toes, gonads to soul,
A man yet ghettoed in Memory's limbo,
Grieving for dead "survivors" like himself,
A child lost in a crowd still gathering,
Still scattering at the Auschwitz depot.

Grodsky the Cobbler

Near the Delmar Loop in St. Louis
(No one knows for sure
In which tenement he dwells),
There lives and dies daily
A Jewish cobbler of shoes,
Who bears just above his bony wrist
Greenish-blue Auschwitz numerals
Obscenely tattooed to his skin
Like an oozing cicatrix,
Shapes crazily misaligned
Like figures floating in alphabet soup.

By trade a shoe repairer,
Anachronous, obsolete,
He still waits — sometimes all day
Without one person in need of his services —
To ply his skills despite near blindness,
Enfeeblement; an octogenarian
Who has no business doing business,
He yet paces sidewalks and crosses streets
As if back in Bremerhaven
Instead of this contemporary American ghetto
Inhabited by blacks, college students, and the elderly,

Where thirty years earlier
The City's most esteemed "kikes" resided —
University professors, symphony musicians,
Bankers, merchants, attorneys, surgeons,
The cream of Midwestern Jewry,
Who, not to their collective face
But always behind their back, were reviled,
Their display windows cracked, cemeteries desecrated —
Spurned because of their learning,
Fenced off by their affluence,
And, finally, betrayed by their success.

Half a century later, lapsing from consciousness,
This ash of a man stoops over his bench,
Apron strings cinching his waist
To keep his pants from falling to his shoes;
Shoes he's repaired so many times
Their original German leather no longer exists,
Nor do their soles remember the shapes
Of the *Vaterland*'s cobbles that wore them smooth
As he fled, his possessions possessed;
Shoes he maintains nonetheless
In case he needs to make another hasty escape.

CHAPTER THREE

PHOENIXES —
SECOND-GENERATION "SURVIVORS"

A Second-Generation "Survivor"

Music from distant spheres seduces my brain
In Katy Station's dim waiting room;
The *Zeitgeist* and poltergeists
Suggest Bergen-Belsen
Flaming in my eyes' nostrils.
I see my father fleeing;
His plight overflows in my mind
Like a clogged toilet someone just flushed.
The pressure exacerbates sensibilities,
Begs release from my hallucination
As I'm transported to Hans Frank's Warsaw Ghetto,
Hungry and bone-cold as dead rats.
Why is this night different from all other nights?
All is gone from the world of light
In which gentle souls caressed,
Illuminating hope with their loving.
Now, bleak anomie seizes me,
A contagious disease
Whose spores multiply inexorably
Until the devastated flesh
Has no more room for infection to flourish.

I strain to reach the strange music's frequency,
Seeking acceptance in its resonance,
But the echoing notes turn a deaf ear
To my petitions for admittance.
I'm left alone in this alien wasteland
Where bartenders and waitresses
Pace like caged leopards and black panthers.
Nothing registers; no faces beckon to me
With even vague recognition.
I shrink, thinking again of the endless procession
Of screeching, straw-strewn boxcars,
And weep as the floor rumbles
With their imminent arrival.
Suddenly, in the distance,
I hear, then see, a steam locomotive
Plangently, ominously making its way toward me
*

Through a rain-bleeding Polish afternoon,
Streaking like Blasco's four apocalyptic riders,
And I realize that my dad's shadow has found me
All these years after the Holocaust,
Hidden beneath the flowing, academic robes
Of Herr Respectable Diogenes Teufelsdröckh,
Professor of Doctrinal Liturgy and Iconohagiography,
Exegetical expert in Dead Sea Scrolls.
Under the black light of this latter-day cabaret,
My yellow-starred armband,
Proclaiming "*Jude*" to the entire purblind world,
Becomes visible. Breathing burns my lungs;
I plunge into the underbrush
Just as a freight train rushes past
En route to dump its contaminated cargo
At the roaring doors of impatient gas chambers.
For now, this time anyway,
I've escaped Fate's palsied hand;
History recriminates over its slight mistake
As I race toward the border
Separating Memory from Today.

By sheer luck, the spectral music abates,
And, like a snake, with just my reflexes,
I begin feeling my way toward Canaan's border,
Toward Sleep,
Just beyond Hades' hoary Gates
That groan open and shut like oven doors
On souls entering this land of transient spirits.
In a matter of moments, my fears explode;
I lay in my bed naked as ancient bones,
Waiting to be claimed, taken home
To the kingdom of God's chosen people,
Home forever to that land
Where men and women thrive without the anxiety
Of being subjugated by demons
Flaunting Schicklgruber mustaches
*

Below Pinocchian noses,
Who make false promises for a livelihood,
Home to the seething womb,
Mother Earth,
Who originally gestated my corpse,
Home again,
Home one final time
In a shrill climax worthy of God's finest creation,
Never to return to this tiny, pendent orb
Again.

Third-Reich Birds

The birds keep an uneasy peace with people —
Even predacious jays
And chicken hawks scanning the sides of highways
For signs of carrion or quick flesh.
Only the crows, their jet-stained contemptuousness
Too ingrained to render them timorous,
Don't flinch at the twitch of a human eye,
Shift of a twig, or leaf-seizure.

Something in their arrogant reflexes,
Numinously or naturally inspired,
Necessarily controls their spectral strategies
To dominate the space they occupy.
Whenever I see one or a *Korps*,
Nearby or at a distance,
My whole body convulses with cold fear;
They have a horrible reputation for breaking treaties.

Deconstructing *Gulliver's Travels*

While driving, getting "blitzed" sipping coffee
And listening to jazz on cassette
To mask voices from the past yet pursuing him,
He progresses his mission to Terra Incognita
In quest of Gulliverian survivors
From the shipwreck that stranded him, too,
Along with captain and crew,
On the sands of a strange Germanic land,
His hands, legs, and tongue tied to a nightmare
From which, despite eventually exiting,
He will never escape.

Today, his trip takes him from St. Louis,
Not Redriff, to Auschwitz, not Lilliput,
To pick up victims or their ghosts,
Who still might wish to piss on the Queen's castle,
Extinguish its Hitlerian firestorm,
And achieve at least symbolic vindication,
If not lasting satisfaction,
For actually having been burned alive
In that conflagration.
Cruising in a caffeine-crazed daze,
He suddenly undiscovers his location in the universe.

Phoenixes

For Menke Katz

My ears almost hear them crisping in the ovens,
Dissipating in acidic attrition
Above Auschwitz,
Entering the ancestral nexus of scripture,
Almost hear them crackling, sputtering,
Lifting into eviscerated whispers
Above the camps,
Almost hear their scattering ashes
Drifting through the blackest atmosphere
Toward the farthest galactic Canaan,
Where hearts beat
And the darkest planets in the sky
Glow like star sapphires backlighted by God
Regardless of man's tragic desires,
His deviations from reason.

My ears can almost hear those Jews,
Who, disguised as smoke, as ash,
Losing all hope,
Refused to die, to die
In me, in my poetry, almost;
Almost, they come to life,
Keep coming alive
As I release them from History
To listen to me listening to them
Weeping for me. Maybe it's not them, either,
But something preternatural
After all — primal fear
Reminding me that I too am a Jew,
Issue of those stillborn
In the hissing wombs of Auschwitz.

Inherited Characteristics

Like a constricting halo,
Dreams weave an insidious spell
About my pulsating brain
As though a megalomaniacal Draco
Has determined to make me his personal slave,

Confine my energies to creating manuscripts
He might offer to foreign powers
In exchange for jet fighters, tanks,
Nuclear missiles, and replacement parts.
Hallucinations barter me for entire arsenals

While nightmares sell me callously
At whatever the going rate of exchange is
At any given moment in the Cosmos,
Dependent only on whim or excessive speculation:
I'm worth at least two radar units,

Three World War II destroyers
Rusting in mothballs,
Five Hellcats or Dauntless dive bombers
Gyved to the rolling decks
Of the Hornet, Yorktown, Wasp, or Enterprise;

My life is easily worth two assaults
On Kwajalein, Iwo Jima, or Corregidor.
My mind is, at any time of the day,
An unprepared Pearl Harbor,
Ripe for utter chaos and destruction.

Even in a waking state, I'm overly anxious
About the potential dilemma
That might arise from my acquiescence
To a barmaid's overtures,
Hoping no one will invite me to celebrate

The end of the most recent war
Between nations ill at ease with each other,
Still uncertain about the outcome of negotiations.
I fear social obligations
Like Super Bowl parties for Howard Cosell,

Bar and Bat Mitzvahs for Muhammad Ali
And Tinker Bell. Whatever the occasion,
I prefer the privacy inherent in ultimate anonymity.
Now I retire to sleep's isolated beachheads
On which my public insecurities fight

And discover my vital statistics on a dog tag
Hanging from Yoko Ono's neck.
The outrageous vagaries increase,
One by two by three to the tenth power
Like a proliferating Polack joke,

And suddenly I recognize myself as the butt
Of a lit Camel-turd cigarette.
My indeterminate location comes into focus
In a Berlin bunker under the Chancellery
Peopled by Goebbels, Himmler, Göring, Bormann,

Eva Braun, and various other demons.
Mortified, I discover I'm the one
With the cropped mustache, star-sapphire eyes,
Malevolent Schicklgruber himself,
Proselytizing with his messianic rhetoric

Zealous fellow Aryans with empty intellects
Imbued with Judeophobia.
Nightmares pale before such stark surrealities.
I die reprising these grotesqueries:
The spell broken dreams weave is my Hell!

Tending the Flock

He's spoken with many survivors
And read memoirs about the dread Scourge
Of the late '30s and early '40s
That virtually extirpated European Jewry;
These interviews have disclosed a verbatim litany
Of ethno-idiosyncratic speeches
Each preaches from his private pulpit,
A collective poetics-manifesto-apologia
Clattering with timidity,
Espousing nonviolent resignation
And faith in a seemingly gratuitous Elohim
Who makes inscrutable promises of *l'chayim*
To His "chosen people."

Always they say the same, lame phrases:
"Unspeakable!";
"It's too shameful to recall";
"I can't remember anything at all
Prior to arriving in the States";
"I died then; only my life survived . . .";
"I don't recognize who I *am*
Or when or why I *was* . . .";
"For years, minutes I've just existed . . .";
"O, the horror —
You can't hide inside it!";
"Silence is the only Resistance group —
I joined it decades ago."

During his informal explorations,
He's recorded testimonies and confessions
That suggest the flock, if diminished,
Is still intact in its vast, scattered corral,
Still vulnerable to mass attacks
From its Gentile shepherds,
Who, in times of plague, inflation, and war,
Would slaughter meek sacrificial lambs
For their meat, skin, and fleece.
This first eve of Pesach,
Sensing his poetry is a sheep's bleat,
He nonetheless coaxes verse from muteness
As though writing like crazy might keep him sane.

A Toast to the Forties, 1985

Like a voracious crow,
Clawing, pecking, hacking at a crimson rabbit
Smashed at the edge of a road,
The wood-slatted ceiling fan above me
Slashes the close, acrid air in Katy Station.

I sit under its pulsating blades,
Vaguely intimidated,
Taking my strained simile
With a superstitious grain of salt,
Discarding, like fast-food packaging
Or Christmas wrapping,
Sinister implications of its poetic correlation.
But as I grow inebriated,
Relaxing within this steamy atmosphere,
Specters of the Holocaust attack me.

Rather than seeing spinning fan blades,
I envision equestrian Time
Viciously wielding his Teutonic scythe,
Victimizing Jews and other miscellaneous detritus
Amidst whose multitude I writhe.

This stained-glass public place,
Where I've frequently wasted placid hours
Imbibing wine, writing sonnets
Before passing out back at my motel,
Becomes a Wagnerian railway station
Crowded with anti-Semitic ghosts:
College-aged Kirchners, Klimts, and Noldes,
Whose overtures of momentary romance
Whisper like passenger trains
Sidetracking my slow-swaying boxcars;

Their swill-brained, lust-filled chatter
Spills onto the hay-strewn floorboard
Of a feces-sullied, destinationless *Lit-wagen*
Through whose sliding door
A Rhine maiden leads me to my booth,
*

After my name is called,
Not to be made whole or clean again by feasting
But to cease breathing, being,
Beneath *Zyklon B* vapors
Descending from a crow-like ceiling fan
Whose talon-blades shred my nostrils.
Why tonight I'm stranded
In this rail-car restaurant eludes me;
Obviously, my soul is no stranger to trains
Racing blindly toward Valhalla.

As though I've not eaten for months, decades,
I'm unable to keep down even one bite.
Hastily, I pay, retreat to the bar,
Where I'm greeted as Death's best patron,
And buy rounds for the Hell of it.

Bringing Klaus Barbie to Trial

How many times must we return
To the scene of our hearts' crimes, dear Lord,
Before learning that cruelty and greed
Are qualities inherent in human doing
And that we repeat our least civilized acts
Not in defense nor from fear for our immortal spirits
But out of a perverse fascination with violence
That transcends infliction of pain on enemies
And disillusionment with those we most adore?

What diabolical impulses exhort us
To explore our darkest desires
By forcing hopeless souls to chew cyanide,
Shoving cowering, naked humans into showers, ovens,
Dismembering breasts, genitalia, vital organs
From those tattooed with the dispersed Tribes' curse
And conceive of breeding a Master Aryan Race
Composed of fair-haired, blue-eyed Teutonics,
Not hooknosed Jewesses and Jews?

Even now, I feel the rails quivering near Dachau,
Though my own senses can only imagine
That clattering death rattle of cattle cars
Crammed with lambs being transported to the slaughter,
Only imagine tasting that acrid blue-black dust
Rising from Auschwitz's factory stacks,
And, although I've visited these Masadas
In a thousand imperishable nightmares and daydreams,
Only imagine their ghosts still roaming Poland.

Is there no end to the genocidal torment of it all?
Can't confession and expiation
Relieve the burden of having to relive it indeterminately
Every time Memory backs up like a flooded gutter
Spewing debris into alleys,
Clogging shortcuts between forgetting and survival?
Why does it persist,
That banshee anthem of damned insanity?
Can't we sentence it to Silence once and forever?

Goddamn Turkey Trucks

Approaching Kingdom City
And running low on fuel,
He exits Highway 70,
Pulls into Gasper's Truck Plaza
To fill both tanks: gas and caffeine.
He goes inside to sign his Visa receipt
Before ordering coffee to go
From a waitress who asks, "Anything in it?"
"No cyanide, please." She's not amused.
Ten feet from the counter, a cashier,
Stationary as a stuffed buffalo,
Blurts out, "70 cents."
"How'd you know?" Feigned amazement
Enhances his sarcasm. "I'm smart."
Chuckling under his breath, he realizes
Just how much he needs cheap talk to keep going.

Buckling up in his station wagon,
He notices he's blocked, front and behind,
By tractor-trailers.
The longer he waits,
The more impatient he grows;
Soon his feet begin to choreograph
An awkward tap dance on the floorboard
While his fingers execute the SOS
Dispatched disasters ago
By the Titanic's radio operator.
Abruptly, he unfastens his seat belt
And jumps out to inspect the disreputable rig
Blocking his forward progress.
The stench blinds him; his nostrils wince.
His senses are confused from the fowl vapors
Wafting into the immediate surroundings

From the Cargill turkey truck
En route from its California, Mo., holding depot
To a processing facility no telling where.
All he knows with certainty
*

Is that these feathers sifting through slats
Of hundreds of interconnected cages
Ain't falling from heaven;
They're more like fiberglass insulation
Blasted into an attic with a pneumatic blower.
No one's in the cab,
And although he's late to nowhere,
This delay is taking its toll.
Just the notion that anything so profane
And outrageously disagreeable
Should stall him on his homeward journey
Is an affront to his dignity.

From some untraceable source in his brain,
He recalls someone once describing
Why turkeys are always jammed so tightly
Into those stacked cages.
He even hears an unidentifiable voice saying,
"They're so fuckin' crazy and dumb,
If ya treat 'em humane,
Ya know, give 'em plenty of space,
They go berserk from blind fear and confusion,
Begin killin' theirselves — no different
Than when ya set domesticated turkeys
Out in the rain: they commence to bunch up
And huddle, all looking straight up,
Lettin' the water fill their nostrils
Until the dumb bastards all drown.
Now that's profoundly ignorant."

As if awakening during a séance,
He takes notice of a burly, bald-headed driver,
Five-foot-five by eight wide,
Wearing cowboy boots, baggy jeans,
And a T-shirt riding up over his beer belly,
Its sleeves exposing his ballooning arms
Graffitied from biceps to wrists with red and blue tattoos
Depicting spread-winged eagles, scrolls,
*

Slogans, hearts, numerals, skulls and crossbones
As in a psychedelic light show.
He watches the man circle his truck,
Then mount and position himself behind the wheel.
Black clots of diesel exhaust
Snort from twin stacks, sully the air
With momentary odors that mask the turkeys' stink;
By degrees, his mind leaves the crime's scene,

But cruising down the road again,
He begins hallucinating, envisioning a train
Tracking across a landscape
He can't place through a warp in time,
A ramshackle locomotive whose throbbing parts —
Valves, pistons, rods, axles, drive shafts,
Pulleys, levers, pumps, and throttling augers —
Might be the mechanisms that keep Hell turning,
A steam engine dragging cattle cars
Packed with faceless human beings
Whose screams and moans catch in the breeze,
Then fade from audible recognition
As they clatter through villages asleep to their passing;
Human beings or turkeys he's not quite certain
For the tightness of their stifled bodies,
Set at 80 to a cage/car

For their own protection, ironically —
An economic decision of the Third Reich —
To guarantee their safe arrival
At a rendering plant/camp
Where, with state-of-the-art expertise,
They might be dispensed with inexpensively
And with no mess whatsoever,
Not even scattered feathers/ashes
Left to be swept up from carriage floors,
Showers, oven maws.
Suddenly he gasps, realizes with a start
He's been following the turkey truck
*

Fifty miles out of his way.
Whether misguided by divine intervention,
Hallucinatory phantasmagoria,
Or his own blind faith,

He doesn't recognize the names of towns
Whose spectral road signs he passes:
Dachau, Mauthausen, Auschwitz-Birkenau.
Where he is he can't fathom.
Fear squeezes him like a boa constrictor;
His breathing collapses in its cold crush,
And he sees no exits
That might let him extricate himself,
Catch his breath, avoid death by asphyxia.
Barely making a severe curve
Where the highway runs alongside a cliff,
Then descends into an endlessly deepening Abyss,
He spies the truck that has led him astray,
Jackknifed, in flames,
Millions of gray-black feathers
Lifting like ashes from its *Yahrzeit* pyre.

The Forest

For Bill Heyen

From a Forest bordering my loneliness,
An amorphous chorus,
Decidedly neither crickets nor known ghosts,
Swells with grotesque moans and groaning.
A sourceless bell knells an elegy
Memory *almost* recognizes.
An obscene smell,
Like the gangrenous guts of a man
Mutilated in a shark frenzy
And stranded on an unending nightmare's shore,
Chokes my nostrils, burns my eyes.
Breathing accelerates;
My heart forgets its place,
Begins echoing millions of others' pulses
As though forming an abhorrent chorus of one
For all those Holocaust dead
God is hoarding
In the Forest bordering my loneliness.

CHAPTER FOUR

THE FINAL DIS-SOLUTION —
Today's Family

Holocaust and Apocalypse

I was recently reborn in an era
When man feared his most violent instincts
Would erupt into corruption
And he'd lose his grip on History,
Trigger genocide,
Explode despair so terrible
That the stench of burning human flesh
Would rise from earth's Auschwitz "strip" mines
And choke everyone for generations on end,
Religious and political expiations
Notwithstanding.
And he did,
By God, by Man, by Damn, he did!

O, what I wouldn't give
To have stayed dead,
Not to have lived to witness
Mankind's sublime indifference
To *Zyklon B* and nuclear fission.
Gladly would I have foregone reincarnation
Just to have missed that incandescence
Over Hiroshima and Nagasaki,
Not to have listened almost fifty years now
To the same blatant smugness
That opened *Enola Gay*'s bomb-bay doors
And sent a strange black dove
Interminably soaring.

But I didn't,
Because I couldn't sidestep Fate
As I tiptoed across Destiny's tightrope.
In fact, with dismaying persuasion,
I was forced to balance atop Satan's shoulders
While supporting on mine
Three other refugees of divorce —
A wife and two dazed children,
Today's manifestation of those earlier exterminations —
As I inched over the Abyss without a net
To catch my Fall. After all,
How could I have been expected to recall
That crucifixion is unalterable for a Christ Killer?

Oblivion

Once, when youthful defiance guided me,
I believed myself immune to persecution;
I'd display indignation
At the slightest sign of racist demonstrations
Or on spying Nazi graffiti
Spray-painted on the faces of limestone cliffs,
Inner-city brick walls,
Fences, cement sidewalks, buses,
And plate-glass skyscrapers
In business districts through whose dizzying mazes
My life maneuvered in those innocent days;
I'd rage, occasionally march or even take the stage,
At political student rallies
And naively speak out against enemies,
Former and current as well as potential,
No matter which radical cause they espoused
To designate them as supporters of the State:
Ku Kluxers, Khrushchevs, Kosygins,
JFKs, LBJs, Nixons,
Stalins, Hitlers, Mussolinis, and Tojos,
Co-conspirators in the War to end all peace,
Down on their knees in allegiance
To Truth subverted, reinvented,
And rented out by the hour to the party in power
Without prior notice or subsequent apologies.

But that was long, long ago,
When growing up brooked no *No*'s
And the only obstacle to my quest for the Grail,
My mission to "change the world,"
Make it bend over backwards and end over end
To accommodate foe and friend
In every ghetto, *shtetl*, Bedouin settlement,
Hobo camp, tent city, Moscow, and Gotham,
Came to me in eerie hallucinations:
Those infrequent nightmares
That focused on atrocities I'd only seen in movies
*

Or read about in books on Auschwitz-Birkenau,
Dachau, Chelmno, and Sachsenhausen,
Places too hellish even for my graphic imagination
To arrest in its earthly verse-cells.
That was all before my self-engendered *Aktion*,
When even those mentions of genocide
Couldn't annihilate my innocent enthusiasm
Despite the disillusionment that gradually developed
After, in my brash and arrogant manner,
I offered myself up,
Highly disciplined body and intellect,
To the Experiment to end all experiments:
Mixed marriage with a lady of Germanic traces
Who gave me a brace of Teutonic children.

Still, at that, the disease took a decade
To reach its flagrant malevolence,
Until one day I realized
Not only would I be unable to rid the world
Of its invidious pretensions, pieties, and bigotry
But, worse, that the phage had overtaken me,
Destroyed my immune system's antibodies
From inside my own house of skin and bones,
Rendering me incapable of saving myself
From the malicious, insidious threats
My wife, and my son and daughter,
Inculcated with her Hitler Youth propaganda,
Were making to me and my life's work as a poet,
Toiling in the sewers, cesspools,
And toxic waste dumps of the human heart
To decry meanness, cruelty, and greed.
Then, one dismal afternoon,
I was paid a visit by two ghostlike strangers
Floating in white trench coats,
Wearing black armbands,
Who grabbed me by the shoulders
And escorted me away, forever, from my house,
*

My neighborhood, city, state, *Vaterland*
To the edge of a jagged Forest
Teeming with thorny locust trees,

Where they stranded me, left me standing naked
For days and years and generations
Until I forgot even the surname
I once wore to clothe myself against the cold.
There I reviewed the cels of my entire life
Fade in the changeless twilight
That bathed me in cyanic vapors
As I stood trembling amidst scattering debris
Emanating from invisible chimneys
I could hear belching and smell —
That nasty, acrid odor of burning flesh —
Those chimneys powering an Unreal City
In an Unreal Universe, with energy to burn.
Then, a more bizarre phenomenon occurred:
I witnessed a vast, vertical tunnel of ash
Spiral in a funnel across the sky,
Elongating, bending at the center
Until its sides came down to the ground
And contained the Earth in a bell jar,
At once opaque and translucent,
From which no elements could escape.
And in that instant,
A single incandescent flash
Shattered the planet, which evaporated,
Leaving only me standing on the edge of Oblivion.

A Case of Mistaken Identities

Flying debris from a cosmic chimney
Pits my corneas with irritants;
Their astringent sting
Makes me wince
As if being whipped by tentacles
Undulating beneath a Portuguese man-of-war
Floating surreptitiously
On an ocean spuming cyanide fumes;
Both eyes feel as though they're burning alive
In an incinerator stoked with human fuel
Or being electrocuted by a broken wire.

Where am I
This blue-eyed St. Louis afternoon
That such sinister visions
Should drift into view,
Distort the image I used to have of you, wife,
Bending so gently into my lips
With a tender kiss?
I no longer recognize your flesh and juices.
Is it conceivable you've mistaken me, too,
Your loving husband,
For Jew-vermin you're about to exterminate?

Race Defilers

Wife, dismissing me so systematically,
You might have been a Nazi Storm Trooper,
And I a "Jew poet" who once saluted your beauty,
Composed your Teutonic essence
In elegies I recited while my books burned,
Burned interminably in Sleep's *Platz*,
Where my dreams, fanned by loneliness,
Stoked nightmarish blazes
Your apostate soul yet ignites in my memory.

For all I know,
Your nymphomaniacal psyche
And gutter-worn physique,
Which used to fit my body and brain
With such Krupp-forged precision,
May always have been a colossal delusion,
An odor rising from my mind's furnaces
Belching at Chelmno,
A smoke puff lifting from a chimney at Auschwitz.

After all, the imagination plays strange tricks on itself,
Formulates such ironic "jews" *de mots*.
Tonight, I envision us
Not divergent but together, as we once were,
Streaking through the universe as fused nebulae
Trying to complete our assigned orbits
Before the entire sky exploded,
Scattered our ashes, as it has, back to shadows,
Buried us in cosmic silence,

Like Adolf and Eva, Mussolini and his Beatrice,
Beneath Dante's charnel-house graveyard.
Finally I see us as we really were: unsainted lovers.
Although you couldn't boast tribal claims
To Old Testament love, nor I worship Christ,
Wife, I take communion tonight
In Loneliness' synagogue —
Your flesh my bread, your blood my wine —
And toast our dream: *Sieg Heil! L'chayim!*

Endlösung

First you laced my imagination,
That garden from which I harvested my nourishment
For more than two decades,
With microscopic parts of arsenic and cyanide;
Next, with infectious, odorless traces of jealousy,
Vituperation, and hatred,
You tainted the wellsprings of my affection
From which our children drank daily.
Then you broke the bottle
With which we toasted the future;
Its toxic vapors fatally asphyxiated me.

Finally, you poured yourself
Into storage drums leaking dioxin,
Agent Orange, PCBs,
Even before they were buried in the Forest.
Still they seep into aquifers and basements
Surrounding the City where I exist —
Auschwitz-on-the-Mississippi —
Which, to this day, glows red at night
From deathless embers of dying memories
Stacked ten rows deep:
Scarecrows outshouting their silent rage.

Today, in a fifty-mile radius,
Emptiness screeches like migrainous sirens;
As though Paradox were mocking me
With its masturbatory echoes,
Throatless klaxons and clangors
From bells lacking clappers
Provoke the shrill stillness
With gentle moans we made making sweet love.
But these days,
The only ghosts in this desolation
Are moles and worms burrowing into my soul.

Desastres de la Guerra

Although the four of us still live together,
I always feel alone at home,
A family man disowned
Even by the ghosts of my own unfaithful wife
And two ungrown children,
Who've followed her into Melancholia's sloughs,
On through Grief's dense forests,
Toward the deepest reaches of Despair,
Where foes and friends are suspended indistinguishably
In sleepless, dazed disillusionment,
Waiting for their turn at vaporous extermination.

In this limbo, I spoon soup
More watery than broth from a child's boot
Protruding from a pile of shoes
Strewn in one corner of a recurring hallucination
And savor a minuscule ration of stale bread,
Gnawing its crust like a rat;
Each chewing movement my taut jaws make
Registers on my emaciated face.
I can taste my bones when they scrape;
They retain a vague flavor of lime
As though they've been buried in Time's mass grave

While I've inhabited this *Lager*-like house
In which my family has lived without speaking to me
For three days. Sadly I realize
That the ghetto of our collapsed marriage,
Whose dehumanization the four of us have suffered
For more than three hysterical years,
Was not the best mode of coexistence;
Being deported to Auschwitz instead
Might have been the lesser of two evils.
No matter, soon forces of Liberation will arrive
To divorce us from the horrors of war.

Spandau, 1989

Quite often in dreams, wife,
I see the bleached carcass of a steer
That strayed in a sandstorm,
Lost its way groping for an oasis
Its bovine divining rod believed existed
Just around the next perpetually bending horizon,
Then gave up hoping to survive,
Reach desert's edge,
Outrace Death's shadow
Stretching to incorporate its own shape,
And arrive intact at a manger
Before the sun's rays
Could holocaust its brain and flesh
In a raging oven
And set its spirit adrift,
Pyring upward
Through Earth's chimney stack
Into acrid winds lifting toward Oblivion.

Quite often, in reality, wife,
I see an emasculated bull
Enduring a state of daily subjugation,
Dying nightly in a dry riverbed,
A victim of the gratuitous cruelty and torment
You've perpetuated committing adultery
And betraying our mixed heritages,
Whose rapid dismantling sent me fleeing
Into a Daliesque desolation, toward a depot
With dissimulating *Lager* gates proclaiming,
"The State of Israel Welcomes You,"
From which I've never escaped,
Waiting for my bones to be thrown into a trench,
Spread with Time-lime,
And decomposed back to stenchless nothingness
With just the memory of your once-gentle touch
To tend my needs and accompany me
Across the Desert of Obliterated Souls.

Till Death Do Us Part: A Personal Holocaust

Why, at this late stage of my life's middle age,
Have I been singled out
To perpetuate my own holocaust?
Wasn't it enough to be chosen Poet
For the ten lost tribes,
Write myself to death in solitude
As though it were a privilege given Moses,
Each poem manna
For survivors of the forty-year trek,
A potato or loaf of bread for Lodz dwellers?
Didn't it suffice that I became an artist,
Relegated to lackluster Ashkeeper,
Archivist of Atrocities and Genocide?

No, that would have been a sentence too lenient,
As would have a marriage of convenience
Between old-foe soul mates
Hellbent on destroying each other;
Just too damned easy
To have elected me leader of the *Judenrat*,
Convinced me to save my skin by betraying friends,
My wife and two offspring,
To dismantle our ghettoed hopes,
Hand them over to *Zyklon B* firemongers.
No! Demanding me to conspire in such cruelties
Only would have banished me
To eternal damnation.

Lord, I see now just how clever You were,
Letting me marry beyond the pale,
Assimilate into the seemingly benign host,
Be deceived by flattering passion,
Love, laughter, youthful dreams,
And lingering beliefs that optimism and faith
Can render all things possible,
Even mixed marriage in a Hitlerian society,
And be lulled out of heeding my two saving graces,
Skepticism and wariness,
*

So that after fathering two children,
I actually forgot to question my dislocation.
And that's when You subjugated my spirit

With her propagandistic doublespeak,
Non-fact, and unaxiomatic truths,
When You canceled my citizenship in the world
And stamped my philosophic and poetic romanticisms
With an indelible Gothic "J,"
Shattering with rocks of scorn and hostility
The shop of cardinal precepts
I deludedly thought we'd shared
In constructing Love from the ground up,
When I became an ostracized member of a "race,"
A dangerous man,
A poet who wrote vermin, not verse,
Capable of perverting and perpetuating

Not-yet-solidified notions of superiority
In certain persons,
Like my no-longer-devoted wife,
Who finally succumbed to her paranoias
Of also being sacrificed
Just because once upon a rainbow ago
She decided to collaborate with me
In sharing our varied lives
Regardless of all potential consequences.
Now her questioning of my heritage,
Her vexatious, perplexing disaffection for me,
Her self-help-book classification
Of every trait I display

Have diminished me to a victim of Satan's deportations,
A living disembodiment
Of a traditional marriage gone defunct,
Smoldering ashes
In the aftermath of my soul's *Kristallnacht* —
That wife who originally set out with me
To fulfill wondrous deeds but succeeded ultimately
*

In decimating every blessed institution
Except her own *Einsatzgruppen*,
Trained to enact one lasting *Aktion*
That will have no equal in my collective Memory:
The execution of her Final Dis-Solution,
Exterminating my spirit from Earth for a thousand years.

Hazards of a Mixed Marriage

I have absolutely no idea when it began
Or first furtively asserted itself —
The Enemy, of course, my adversary,
My wife of so many anniversaries,
Hiding benignly inside our citadel
All those years of our early romance,
Through the blessed birthing of two children,
Blue-eyed, blond boy and girl,
So exquisitely robust, so precocious —

When it first decided to bare its teeth,
Brandish its clawed paws,
And shadowbox in the mirror,
Scowling menacingly for some *Mein Kampf* effect
It was already subconsciously formulating
And preparing to unloose on my unsuspecting universe,
No idea when she began seeing the Gentile,
Sneaking into bars and bed with him,
Sanctifying adultery as her Catholic birthright.

To this day, with nauseating lucidity,
I can recall last Christmas Eve,
When she gifted me with two mezuzahs
Because I'd "become so Jewish lately,"
She cynically said with a sinister intent
I even then intuited meant the beginning of the end
Of our defense against the Enemy
We'd always heard hissing
Behind the portcullis of our sandcastle fortress.

I listened to her *Protocols of the Elders of Zion*,
Issuing unpredictably from her lips,
Heard her unsympathetic edicts
Limiting my freedom to pursue my chosen vocation,
Composing poetry (it was a profession too impecunious
To sustain her "nouveau Reich" lifestyle),
Bore witness all too frequently
To her evenings out for "Beer Hall" meetings
"Party members" required her to attend;

I saw her leave the house in sheer blouses
Or T-shirts and designer jeans,
Festooned with garish necklaces,
Meretricious bracelets and dangling earrings,
With satin roses in her whore-hair,
Reeking of sickly sweet almond perfume,
And return in the dead of my nightmares
Like a phantom snake slithering up each stair
To her separate bedroom, oblivious of my existence

Or, if not, insidiously all too aware,
In fact, ready at that time
To annihilate me, expunge my meager influence
On children she'd already intoxicated
With her Teutonic doctrines of distaff superiority
Until one night last month, in the kitchen,
She seethed, "Get those out of this house;
Have them sent to your office from now on."
Too stunned to weep, I quit eating,

Then fled, taking my coat, attaché,
And the newspapers my wife had just desecrated,
Copies of the *St. Louis Jewish Light*,
One of which contained a profile of me
Along with other local writers.
"And take those fucking mezuzahs, too";
These last words she hurled at the back of my head
Were ashes still flashing in a massive oven.
To this day, my scars are open arteries.

The Final Dis-Solution

This dismal day, I awaken disturbingly early
In my pay-by-the-day motel room
As if still relegated to a Jew-ghetto
Not by Nazis but God's marauding Storm Troopers,
Wrenched out of bed in my pajamas,
Dispossessed of trappings
That fortified me
For more than a quarter of a century.
Ripped from dreams throbbing like a cut carotid,
I feverishly try to identify my surroundings,
This emotional emptiness without hope,
Love, happiness, passion, or faith,
But no place markers are familiar;
I'm lost behind barbed fences
And cell bars, beneath sewer grates.

Suddenly I diagnose the etiology of my malaise:
Invading microbes constituting the plague
That nightly levels Sleep's inner city
Emanate from you, phantom wife.
You've polluted my future
With your dissolute cruelty
And hellish infidelity;
Your worm has eaten its way
To the core of my cerebrum,
Formed a crust of death-spores over Memory.
Separated from you, I exist yet in a cosmic firestorm,
Forever bereft, inconsolably restless —
Though we're about to be divorced,
Your Storm Troopers
Still violate my borders with impunity.

Celebrating Her Deathday

From the outset of our mixed marriage,
For fear of being assimilated,
We fled as far from civilization
As we dared without completely removing ourselves
From our Catholic and Jewish heritages,
Raised two ecumenical children
And lived, *almost* happily ever after,
In a white clapboard, high-Victorian castle
Overlooking Smalltown, America,
Where I and she, my former wife and friend,
Would seize the perennial opportunity
To squeeze all hues from the tube
And paint the town crazy with rainbows
Just to celebrate her nativity.

But today, my awakening is a wake,
Not another birthday of hers
I might, these days, only in a fugue,
Be tempted to commemorate by lifting my cup,
Whispering vestigial *l'chayim*'s.
Quite the contrary, I maintain hatred for her,
The one who rent our wedding vows,
Made our children brain-dead to me
For the remainder of their adolescence, possibly forever,
By previewing for them nightly,
Beginning years before she finally phoned the Gestapo
And had them rip me from our bed,
Her Riefenstahl-styled version of Teutonic propaganda
Calculated to increase her inferior self-esteem;

She with those beguiling, Rhine-maiden wiles
Too devious to defense, like V-2 rockets
Screaming out of a night sky over Blighty;
She whose birthday once occurred for me
With boisterous joy,
Regularly as the cuckoo bird
That pecked open its swinging doors hourly
To play its two-note concerto —
*

That Black Forest pendulum clock
I gifted her one birthday for good luck,
Which hovered like a crucifix over our kitchen table,
Where the four of us broke fast daily.
Today, it's packed away in a box or lost;
But I may yet decide to celebrate — her *Yahrzeit*.

An American Holocaust

The pain of having my children seized from me
Is more excruciating than being caught
In a rain of white-hot ash
Dropping from Bergen-Belsen's chimney stacks
Bellowing nonstop into a gaseous welkin:

Those two blessed souls
I've been so devoted to since their births,
Now subverted through distaff propaganda,
Ghettoed from their father's love and companionship,
And sent alone into the Unknown.

O, the emptiness! My silently violent grief
Is a ceaseless screeching of eagles
That nearly cancels my heart's frantic beating.
Oxygen has stopped irrigating my garden,
Whose seeds rot under Time's lime.

But the greatest pain is witnessing them
From this distance not even Imagination can bridge
For the dense fencing my wife has erected
And spliced with Nazi hostility,
Envisioning them dying in her barbed-wire vengeance.

The Pawnbrokers

Even before I get my first words out
This City-fleeing morning,
Set in sequence chaos-slaking cadences
Metamorphosing magically
Into stanzaic patterns on blue-ruled pages,
My eyes well up with invisible tears
Intellect evokes from its image-bottle
By unstoppling throttled grief
Festering in Memory's flask:
Sadness elicited just whispering "Nazerman";
His name is a fist hitting me in the throat.
I gasp the typhus-infested air
He breathed at Auschwitz,
Witness visions afflicting him all his days:
Gnarled, palsied hands clinging to Cyclone fences
As Nazis rip rings from arthritic fingers;
German shepherds chewing shoes,
Cuffs of striped uniforms, and human-leg flesh
Of those courageously stupid few,
His best friend included, who tried to escape;
Women brutally raped; multitudes of naked ciphers,
Identified only by blue numerals,
Moaning, dying in communal loneliness and pain.

Driving away from his postwar New Jersey,
My St. Louis, I listen to his cataleptic voice,
Buried alive in a grave
Packed with ossifying bones
Ten thousand thousand lives deep,
Wanting to scream that he wished he'd died then, too,
Questioning "Why not me?
How could the Grim Reaper have missed me
With his sickle-bar scythe?"
I hear the quivering voice of that man called "Uncle"
By those waifs relying on his misbegotten existence
To deliver them, somehow, from destitution,
He whom they also called "usurer,"
*

"Dirty Jew," "greedy Hebe," "kike";
That sick-to-his-soul victim
Of his own ubiquitous, lacerated hallucinations
Finally vanquishing silence
Long enough to answer Jesús Ortíz,
His Harlem-born, Hispanic assistant,
By formulating a curt reply
To the innocent inquiry about the numbers above his wrist —
"Hey, Mister Nazerman,
Do you belong to a secret society?"
"Secret society? . . . O, yeah."
"Well, how do *I* belong?"
"How do *you* belong, Jesús?" he mimics,
Pausing as if staring into Irony's fire-breathing nostrils.
"Yes, teacher."
"You walk on water, *that's* how!"

Watching the blue ink dripping from my pen,
I fill with a chill so hot
Goose pimples dot my skin,
Then the ink becomes my blood;
I feel it leaking out of my veins
Into Sol Nazerman's constricted circulatory system,
Nourishing his haunted, impoverished spirit,
And the transference occurs before my eyes:
I see him as the father he was,
Before Storm Troopers abruptly invaded
And ruptured the quietude he shared
With his wife and two beautiful children —
Those last quarter-time picnic scenes
In which the four of them are cavorting in a field,
Engaged in a seemingly endless, peaceful play
Of spirited innocence;
I see this tableau gratuitously shattered,
His two children killed
By an unsuspected intrusion of barbarian hordes
Wresting, molesting, exterminating
*

In one burnished, swastikaed eagle's fell swoop
All his cultivated ambitions, dreams,
And hopes of furthering his *Vaterland*'s glory
By adding to it his own proudly conceived progeny.

Suddenly I see *my* two children,
Gone in a blink, like Nazerman's,
And now I see myself retreating from St. Louis
Forty years after his cinematic exodus,
Bereaved, eviscerated, nonexistent,
A bottomless well of echoing black stagnation
Whose spouse might have been Solly's foe,
An entire demented nation in one adulterous wife
Who would deny him his fundamental human rights,
Deprive him of even seeing his children,
Both teenagers now,
By poisoning them with her Goebbels-like insinuations,
That propagandistic litany she used
To slander him for her misdeeds,
Make them believe her Germanic blood
Was Aryan-pure despite having made their marriage
A "mixed" one many times over
To satisfy her sexual and chemical addictions.

Nazerman, you poor, sad bastard,
I hear you, see you this horrific morning,
But for inscrutable reasons,
Though I identify with you, your plight,
I'm unable to express my sympathy
Not because, at fifty, I feel *your* desecration
Is no longer so extraordinary to me —
No, not, I believe, because *your* suffering
And failure to achieve, even through numbness,
A consolation approximating inner peace
Exceeds any catastrophe deserving compassion —
But rather because I, too, am, like you,
Empty of sentiment, effaced,
Incapable of generating feelings of pity or sorrow
*

Even for myself, let alone for another.
Solly! Uncle! Professor! Kike Nazerman!
Rod Steiger! Sydney Lumet!
L. D. Brodsky!
Can you hear me? I'm the Diaspora-guy,
The poet, stranded out here
On this road going nowhere endlessly —
I am the very blue ink I apply
To create from my wrinkled fingers and wrist
These eerie strokes, *my* blue numerals,
Identifying my spirit's membership
In Life's secret society.
Won't someone deliver me from this desolation,
Show me the right exit from this highway
I've been driving now
How many wildernesses wide I don't even know?
Won't someone show me how to turn ink into water
And, if not how to walk on it,
At least, by reading between my lines, part it
And show me how to pass unscathed
Through my heart's Red Sea?

Epilogue

My Holocaust Flowers

Although I didn't realize it then,
The seeds of my Holocaust poems
Had already been german-ating
In Imaginations's beds
Long before their first roots burrowed down
And undernourished shoots
Thrust upward through loose dirt,
Budding open into brown-edged doom-blooms,
Long before Youth's dew evaporated.

Now, it's been nearly a decade
Since these *fleurs du mal* —
The earliest resembling erikas, begonias,
Impatiens, violets, and crotons,
Profuse in their tightly bunched clumps
Like sarcomatous lumps in a rumbling lung —
Began appropriating plots
I'd tilled to fill with other designs.
I still don't know who planted those seeds,

Whether or not a kind of divine madness
Was behind the original idea,
Or why I, a tribal scribe
Bent on recording gentler colors and signs,
Should have been chosen
To tend such an adventitious creation.
But O, the hours I've spent
Hoeing, weeding, pruning,
Fertilizing them with hallucinatory oracles!

If, in the beginning, I'd only known
These flowers would require a lifetime
To keep them from dying out,
I'd never have allowed them to grow,
Taken them into my house, made bouquets,
Placed them in crystal vases,
*

And misted them daily,
Obsessed with seeing how long they'd survive.
But how could a poet know

That being "Chosen" was really no honor,
Instead, an obligation
By default of God Himself,
A vocation he'd not be able to evade?
Even now, each early a.m.,
I go outside my dreams, pace the beds —
They're as large as Versailles' gardens —
And try to decide which flowers I'll pick
To place on my grave that day.

Biographical Note

Louis Daniel Brodsky was born in St. Louis, Missouri, in 1941, where he attended St. Louis Country Day School. After earning a B.A., Magna Cum Laude, at Yale University in 1963, he received an M.A. in English from Washington University in 1967 and an M.A. in Creative Writing from San Francisco State University the following year.

From 1968 to 1987, while writing poetry continuously, he managed a 350-person men's clothing factory and developed for Biltwell Co., Inc. of St. Louis, Missouri, one of the Midwest's first factory outlet chains.

Mr. Brodsky has coedited eight scholarly books on Nobel laureate William Faulkner and authored a biography titled *William Faulkner, Life Glimpses*. He is the author of nineteen volumes of poetry, five of which are currently being translated for French publication by Éditions Gallimard.

Also available from **Time Being Books**

LOUIS DANIEL BRODSKY
You Can't Go Back, Exactly
The Thorough Earth
Four and Twenty Blackbirds Soaring
Mississippi Vistas: Volume One of *A Mississippi Trilogy*
Forever, for Now: Poems for a Later Love
Mistress Mississippi: Volume Three of *A Mississippi Trilogy*
A Gleam in the Eye: Poems for a First Baby

LOUIS DANIEL BRODSKY and WILLIAM HEYEN
Falling from Heaven: Holocaust Poems of a Jew and a Gentile

ROBERT HAMBLIN
From the Ground Up: Poems of One Southerner's Passage
   to Adulthood

WILLIAM HEYEN
Erika: Poems of the Holocaust
Pterodactyl Rose: Poems of Ecology
Ribbons: The Gulf War — A Poem

RODGER KAMENETZ
The Missing Jew: New and Selected Poems

TIME BEING BOOKS
POETRY IN SIGHT AND SOUND
Saint Louis, Missouri

10411 Clayton Road • Suites 201-203
St. Louis, Missouri 63131
(314) 432-1771

TO ORDER TOLL-FREE
(800) 331-6605 Monday through Friday, 8 a.m. to 4 p.m. Central time
FAX: (314) 432-7939

Please call or write for a free catalog.